FIESTA!

IRAN

GROLIER

An Imprint of Scholastic Library Publishing
Danbury, Connecticut

Published for Grolier,
an imprint of Scholastic Library Publishing
Old Sherman Turnpike, Danbury, Connecticut 06816
by Times Editions,
an imprint of Times Media Pte Ltd

Copyright © 2004 Times Media Pte Ltd, Singapore
First Grolier Printing 2004

Set ISBN: 0-7172-5788-6
Volume ISBN: 0-7172-5794-0

Library of Congress Cataloging-in-Publication Data
Iran.
p. cm.—(Fiesta!)
Summary: Discusses the festivals and holidays of Iran and how the songs, food,
and traditions associated with these celebrations reflect the culture of the people.
1. Festivals—Iran—Juvenile literature. 2. Iran—Social life and customs—Juvenile literature.
[1. Festivals—Iran. 2. Holidays—Iran. 3. Iran—Social life and customs.]
I. Grolier (Firm). II. Fiesta! (Danbury, Conn.)
GT4874.A2I73   2004
394.2655—dc21   2003044840

For this volume
Author: Shabnam Gholamrezaei
Editor: Melvin Neo
Designer: Lynn Chin
Production: Nor Sidah Haron
Crafts and Recipes produced by Stephen Russell

Printed in Malaysia

Adult supervision advised for all crafts and recipes,
particularly those involving sharp instruments and heat.

CONTENTS

IRAN

Known to the world as Persia until the 1950s, Iran lies to the northeast of the Persian Gulf. The country was once the center of the Persian Empire (559–330 B.C.), which stretched from northern India to Greece.

CASPIAN SEA

TEHRAN

IRAQ

Esfahan

Persepolis

KUWAIT

SAUDI ARABIA

Persian Gulf

QATAR

◄ **Tehran,** the capital of Iran, is home to many grand palaces built by Persian royalty throughout history. The Golestan Palace is special because it houses the *Takht-e-Taavous,* or the Peacock Throne. The throne is made of gold and decorated with jewels.

TURKMENISTAN

AFGHANISTAN

PAKISTAN

Gulf of Oman

UNITED
ARAB
EMIRATES

◄ **Miniature paintings** are a special Iranian art form. The paintings are very colorful and intricate. Artists who produce miniature paintings are admired for their creativity as well as their keen eyesight, steady hands, and great patience.

▲ **The griffin** is a mythical bird-like creature and a Persian symbol of strength, vigilance, and peace. The griffin has the head and wings of an eagle and the body of a lion. The Persian name for the griffin is *Homa.*

► **Tea** is a favorite drink in Iran, and it is always served hot without milk or sugar. Sugar cubes, however, are provided on the side for those who want a taste of sweetness with their drink. In Iran people do not stir sugar into their tea. Instead, they place the sugar cubes on their tongues before sipping hot tea to melt the sugar cubes in their mouths.

RELIGIONS

Iran is the only country in the world where Shi'ite Islam is the official religion. All other Islamic countries follow Sunni Islam. Sunni and Shi'ite are the two main branches of Islam. All Muslims, however, believe that there is only one God, Allah, and that Muhammad is his prophet.

THE DIFFERENCE between the Shi'ites and the Sunnis is that the Shi'ites only recognize the descendants of Prophet Muhammad as their leaders. Sunnis, on the other hand, accept people unrelated to Prophet Muhammad to be their leaders.

Shi'ites identify their religious leaders, called *imam*, not only by name but also by numbers. The number marks the *imam's* closeness to Muhammad. Imam Ali, the Prophet's son-in-law, is the first *imam*. Hassan and Hossein, Ali's sons, are regarded as the second and third *imams*.

Except for who the two groups regard as *imams*, the Shi'ites follow the same practices as the Sunnis. The Qur'an (Koran) is the holy book for all Muslims, and their place of worship is called a mosque. All Muslims follow certain rules. For example, they do not eat pork or drink alcohol.

Islam has five main ideas, called the Five Pillars, that all Muslims follow.

The first pillar, called the *shahadah*, is a declaration of faith by a Muslim. It states, "There is no God but Allah and Muhammad is His messenger." The second pillar, called the *salat*, tells the people to pray to Allah five times a day. The third pillar, called *saum*, requires Muslims to fast during the holy month of Ramezan. The fourth pillar, called *zakat*, urges Muslims to donate to those who are poor. The fifth pillar is called *haj*, or pilgrimage. All Muslims try to make a pilgrimage to the holy city of Mecca in Saudi Arabia at least once in their lives.

Since Islam does not allow the depiction of humans and other living objects, religious objects often take the form of elaborate writing called calligraphy.

GREETINGS FROM **IRAN**

Most Iranians speak the Persian language, also known as Farsi. It is also spoken in Afghanistan, Bahrain, Iraq, and Oman. Iran has a population of over 66 million. About half are Persian, and a quarter are Azerbaijanis. Gilakis, Mazandaranis, and Kurds form the largest minority groups, with about 8 percent each. Arabs, Lors, Baluchis, and Turkmen make up what is left of the population, at about 1 percent. In Iran 89 percent of the population are Shi'ite Muslims, while 10 percent are Sunni Muslims. The remaining Iranians are Zoroastrians, Christians, and Jews. Zoroastrianism is an ancient religion whose main idea is that all the good forces in the world are united under one God. This God, known as Ahura Mazda, is the creator of the universe, heaven, hell, and all things in them. Although Iran is an Islamic state today, Zoroastrianism's influence is visible in many parts of Iranian culture. In fact, many festivals involve a blend of practices.

How do you say...

Hello
Salaam

How are you?
Haale shoma chetoreh?

Goodbye
Khoda-hafez

Thank you
Mersi

You are welcome
Khaahesh mikonam

Peace
Solh

CHAHAR-SHANBEH SOORI

This festival takes place on the last Tuesday of the Iranian calendar. The name of the festival, Chahar-Shanbeh Soori, literally means the "eve of Wednesday celebrations" in Farsi.

The calendar in Iran is based on the movements of the sun. The Iranian year begins on either March 20 or 21. The exact day depends on the time of the spring equinox.

Chahar-Shanbeh Soori is held on the last Tuesday of the Iranian year. During Chahar-Shanbeh Soori bonfires are lit all over the country, and people jump over them. Each jump symbolically closes the old year. The jump also welcomes the new year with hope and many good wishes.

Many people will also recite the chant — *Sorkhi-e to az man, Zardi-e man az to* ("Give me your beautiful red color and take back my sickly pallor"). During this time a rich and thick soup called *Ash* is also often eaten at dinner.

Although this festival originated from ancient Zoroastrian beliefs, the

During Chahar-Shanbeh Soori children dress up in new clothes. People also serve snacks such as walnuts to guests.

AJEEL E CHAHAR SHANBEH SOORI

This mixture of dried fruit, nuts, and sweets is a must-have for *Chahar-Shanbeh Soori*. The mixture represents the "untangling of knots" or the "solving of problems." The seven ingredients form the basic mixture, to which Buslogh or sugar figs are added. Buslogh is a sugar-dusted, chewy sweet with chopped walnuts in the middle. Sugar figs are sweets made from castor sugar to look like figs.

YOU WILL NEED
½ cup pistachios
½ cup roasted chickpeas
½ cup almonds
½ cup hazelnuts
½ cup figs
½ cup apricots
½ cup raisins

1 Measure equal amounts of pistachios, roasted chickpeas, almonds, hazelnuts, figs, apricots, and raisins, and pour into a large mixing bowl.

2 Toss the ingredients to ensure that they are evenly mixed.

3 Serve as is, or add a few pieces of Buslogh or sugar figs.

way it is celebrated today reflects a blend of Islamic influences. In the past the children would wear shrouds, and they would walk through the streets, going from door to door.

The appearance of the children is supposed to signify the returning spirits of their deceased family members. At every home they visit the children are offered a sweet treat called *Ajeel e Chahar Shanbeh Soori*. It is a mixture of seven types of dried fruit and nuts — roasted chickpeas, pistachios, almonds, figs, hazelnuts, raisins, and apricots.

In recent times the strong Islamic influences have seen Wednesday as an unlucky day. To prevent Chahar-Shanbeh Soori from being outlawed by the government, Iranians have invented an extra feature: that of banging on pots and pans with spoons. It is said that the noise chases away the bad luck that comes with Wednesday.

Iranians make loud noises by banging on pots and pans to "frighten" away the bad luck that comes on Chahar-Shanbeh Soori.

NORUZ

The Iranian version of New Year's Day, Noruz begins on the first day of the Iranian calendar with festivities lasting for twelve days.

The moment of the spring equinox is called *Tahvil* in Iran. On the first day of Noruz, when *Tahvil* takes place, every Iranian family observes a special custom.

All family members gather around a special arrangement of seven items. This display is called the *Haft Sin*. All the seven items selected have names that begin with an "s" sound, and they are of religious or cultural significance.

The items of the *Haft Sin* are *seeb* (apple), which represents health and

An apple (above), coins, and garlic (opposite) are just some of the items that make up the Haft Sin.

beauty; *senjed* (dried lotus fruit), which represents love; *sek'keh* (coins), which represents wealth and prosperity; *sir* (a clove of garlic), which represents health; *serkeh* (vinegar), which represents old age and patience; *samanu* (a paste made from wheat germ), which is regarded as holy; and *sumac* (a sour tasting spice made from berries), whose red color represents goodness and new life.

Several other items that are not part of the *Haft Sin* are also new year favorites among Iranians. These are *laleh* (tulips) and *sonbol* (hyacinth) to represent spring; *sabzeh* (wheatgrass) to represent

During celebrations for Noruz, Iranians serve pastries and tea to their visitors. The tea leaves are kept in beautiful containers such as the one on the left.

book of poetry. Hafez and Sdadi are famous poets in Iran.

Noruz is a celebration of rebirth and renewal. Therefore, it is important that everything related to this festival is new or clean. This includes people's clothing and shoes, and even household items. That is why for weeks before Noruz Iranians rigorously clean their homes. Iranians take this

period of cleaning very seriously. In fact, spring-cleaning in Farsi is *khaneh tekaani*, which literally means "shaking house."

This tireless cleaning is a way for Iranians to capture spring's spirit of rebirth or renewal — by cleaning out the old year and getting ready for the new. During cleaning, old and worn household items are often thrown out and replaced with new ones.

rebirth; goldfishes to represent life; a mirror to remind one to reflect; candles to represent light and goodness; colored eggs to represent the fertility of the people and their land; and a book to represent wisdom. The book used can be the Qur'an (the Islamic holy book) or the Avesta (the Zoroastrian holy book). Some Iranians may use a

11

Children adore Noruz because they get to wear new clothes and shoes. They also receive money, in the form of crisp new notes, and presents from older family members.

Iranians spend the first few days of the New Year visiting family and friends. It is customary for younger family members to begin Noruz by visiting those older than them, starting with the oldest family member. For example, Iranians visit their great-grandparents (if they are still living) before their grandparents and their grandparents before their uncles and aunts. By the end of the twelve-day period the older members of the family would have also visited those younger than them in return.

Traditional Iranian beliefs state that the way people start the new year will decide how the rest of the year will be for them. That is why Iranians prefer to start the year with family and friends. Bad feelings are forgotten, and any two people upset with each other

usually make up on this day. Over the years this custom led to the creation of Haji Firouz, a jolly, middle-aged character.

Haji Firouz is to Noruz just as Santa Claus is to Christmas. Always dressed in red, Haji Firouz walks through Iranian streets announcing the arrival of the new year. Men who

Iranians dress modestly and keep their bodies covered according to Islamic traditions.

play Haji Firouz typically have their faces and hands painted black with make-up. The actors perform comical acts and sing while tapping on the tambourine. In times past, slaves of African descent were often asked to play Haji Firouz. That is because while children tended to giggle at the unfamiliar accents, they were also attracted by them. Iranian

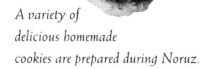

A variety of delicious homemade cookies are prepared during Noruz.

parents would give lavish gifts and money to Haji Firouz for bringing the good news of spring to their families.

Elaborate and colorful feasts are held during the season. The year's first evening meal is called *Sabzi Polo Mahi.* It consists of rice cooked with fresh herbs and pieces of fish. Another Iranian dish, called *Kokou Sabzi,* often accompanies *Sabzi Polo Mahi,* and it is made from various vegetables, eggs, and plenty of fresh herbs.

DARA'S SONG

Sah-rah gol-eh Sah- rah bood   Een Dohk-ta-reh zih-baw bood

Har-jaw keh reh-sahd paw-yash   Mih-roo-yahd az on-jmaw gol

A CELEBRATION OF KING JAMSHID

The great Persian poet Ferdowsi wrote an epic poem called Shahnamah. It tells the story of how Noruz celebrations originated from King Jamshid, a mythical figure.

LEGEND HAS IT that King Jamshid was a great man and ruler. During his reign Jamshid captured the demons and turned them into slaves who helped build houses for the people. The king invented iron weapons and armor to protect his kingdom. He also refined ways of making medicine, clothes, jewelry, and perfume to improve life in his kingdom.

King Jamshid divided his people into four groups that each looked after a part of life. The priests devoted their lives to God and ensured the spiritual wellness of the people. The warriors protected the land. The farmers produced food that fed the people. Last, the craftsmen provided shelter for the people.

King Jamshid was blessed with *Farr-e-Izadi*, which is a special grace and power given by God. With *Farr-e-Izadi* a ruler is immortal for as long as he is kind and fair to his people.

Since the king excelled at everything he did, there came a day when he was declared to be the master of everything except the heavens. Jamshid, however, wanted to reach even the heavens and ordered the craftsmen to design a throne decorated with jewels. When the throne was completed, Jamshid sat on it and ordered his slaves to lift him up toward the heavens. They pushed Jamshid higher and higher into the sky, until the sun's rays shone directly on the throne. At that point a bright burst of colors filled the sky. To celebrate the event, the people showered King Jamshid with even more jewels. The day was marked as *Noruz*, meaning "new day," and recognized as the first day of the year.

The king would have been immortal had he not allowed his power to corrupt him. Soon Jamshid believed that there was no one greater than himself. One day the king told his people that because his special power gave him total control over their lives and deaths, they should regard him as the Creator of the World.

The king's arrogance led to his downfall. Jamshid lost his *Farr-e-Izadi*, and no matter how hard Jamshid begged God to return him to his former glory, God would not listen.

WHEATGRASS GROWING

Wheatgrass is an important symbol during the Iranian new year and is almost always seen beside the *Haft Sin*. *Sabzeh*, or wheatgrass, is later discarded on *Seezdeh be dar*, or the thirteenth day of the new year.

YOU WILL NEED

A small handful of wheatgrass seeds
A drinking glass
A dinner plate
2–3 pieces of paper towel
Colander/sieve

1 Soak wheatgrass seeds in a glass of water for 24 hours.

2 Drain seeds by emptying the contents of the glass into a colander or sieve.

3 Put a piece of paper towel on top of the plate. Then, empty the contents of the colander or sieve onto the paper towel.

4 Cover the seeds with another piece of paper towel, and sprinkle water generously over the top. Then, put everything in the shade for 24 hours.

5 Sprinkle lots of water over the top of the paper towel until the seeds are damp.

6 Leave everything in the shade for another 24 hours.

7 Uncover the top piece of paper towel, and the sprouts should be about $1/4$ inch tall and off-white in color. Replace paper towel, and sprinkle water over the top. Keep in the shade for another 24 hours.

8 Remove the paper towel, and the sprouts should be about $1/2$ inch tall and a little greenish. Put the plate in a sunny spot, and water once or twice a day to keep roots damp. Wheatgrass will grow taller and greener by the day.

SEEZDEH BE DAR

The first month of the Iranian calendar is called Farvardin. On the thirteenth day of Farvardin the people celebrate Seezdeh Be Dar.

After the Noruz celebrations it is common for the people to spend as many hours as possible outdoors.

On the thirteenth day of the new year Iranian families head to the parks to have lavish picnics. The picnics feature a wide selection of breads, cheeses, fresh herbs, and fruit. Wealthy Iranians will visit their summer homes, which are located in the surrounding highlands, during this time.

Seezdeh Be Dar is another instance of how Iranians have blended Zoroastrian traditions and Islamic influences over time. In Zoroastrianism every day is considered sacred and is associated with a particular deity. On the thirteenth day of Farvardin the deity is Tishtrya, the protector of rain. Before the rise of Islam Iranians celebrated the day with outdoor festivities relating to rain.

In the early days the people's livelihood depended on agriculture. During the festivities the people prayed for rain to ensure that their crops get enough water.

During Seezdeh Be Dar Iranians have picnics in the parks. Salads and goat cheese are some of the items included in the picnic basket.

Iranian handicrafts are of a very high quality, as can be seen in this water container (left) and jewelry box (below).

With the rise of Islam in Iran, however, every thirteenth day was seen as unfavorable and full of bad luck. Emerging from a mixture of the two religions, Iranians today regard going outdoors on the thirteenth day as the only way to avoid the bad luck that would otherwise befall them. By spending the entire day outdoors, Iranians also get a chance to practice some ancient Zoroastrian customs, such as throwing *Sabzeh* (wheat-grass) into rivers or streams. It is also a part of Iranian customs for unwed girls to tie a knot with any two green shoots if they want to be married that year.

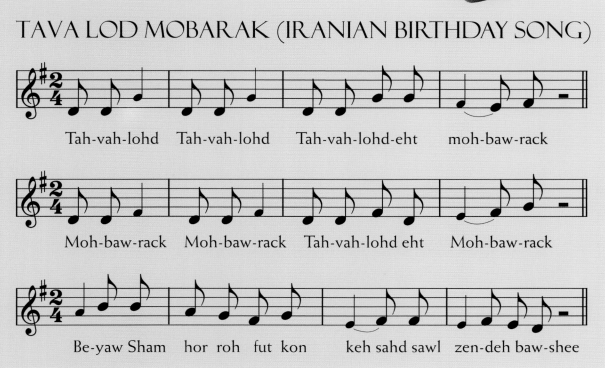

TAVA LOD MOBARAK (IRANIAN BIRTHDAY SONG)

Tah-vah-lohd   Tah-vah-lohd   Tah-vah-lohd-eht   moh-baw-rack

Moh-baw-rack   Moh-baw-rack   Tah-vah-lohd eht   Moh-baw-rack

Be-yaw Sham   hor roh fut kon   keh sahd sawl   zen-deh baw-shee

SHAB-E-CHELEH

In December, which is the ninth month of the Iranian calendar, the people observe an event called Shab-e-Cheleh.

The winter solstice, the longest night of the year, falls on December 21 or 22. In the Iranian calendar December is the ninth month of the year, and it is called Azar. The last day of Azar, which falls on the winter solstice, is when Iranians gather with family and friends to mark Shab-e-Cheleh.

Fires are lit and kept burning all night at this time. That is because in the past Iranians believed that the forces of darkness were strongest then as a result of the long hours of darkness. The fires were supposed to represent the people's faith in the triumph of good over evil, light over darkness.

Based on the principles of Zoroastrianism, the

After the feasts end on the day of the winter solstice, Iranian families gather together with their friends to read from books of poetry.

battle between good and evil was thought to be created by Ahura Mazda, the Lord of Wisdom. The evil force was called Ahriman, and the people feared his power, which was strongest at this time.

The people hoped that Shab-e-Cheleh would pass peacefully into the next day, called Khoram Rooz.

Zoroastrians believe that the first day of the tenth Iranian month, called Day, is protected by Ahura Mazda. As the month of Day passes, nights become shorter and shorter. The ancient Iranians, who believed in Zoroastrianism, held celebrations to honor Ahura Mazda's protection

Since the Iranian lifestyle used to be very dependent on agriculture, seasonal fruits such as pomegranate (right) and watermelon (below) are traditionally eaten at Shab-e-Cheleh.

of the people from evil.

Iranians today, while mostly Muslim, also observe Shab-e-Cheleh with some festivity, but there is little religious significance. These days the festival is seen as a time for family and friends to get together.

Iranians typically hold huge feasts, which must include a vast array of nuts and dried and seasonal fruit, such as pomegranate and watermelon. This is, again, another Zoroastrian

tradition handed down through the years when the people's lives and sources of food depended on agriculture.

For early Iranians, to gather both dried and fresh fruit and nuts was a gesture representing their thanks and their prayers to the deities, who they believed watched over their winter crops. At the end of the feast it is also customary for family members and their friends to recite poetry, which include works by Hafez and other great writers.

IRANIAN PAPER CUTOUTS

Paper cutouts are a popular hobby in Iran. The designs produced can range from simple patterns to those with many folds and cuts. Cutouts are often used as a form of decoration in the home.

YOU WILL NEED
Colored paper
A pair of sharp scissors

A BUTTERFLY

1 Fold the colored paper in half to form a triangle as seen in the diagram. The colored side should be on the inside.

2 Trace the pattern shown on the left onto the triangle.

3 Using the scissors, carefully cut away the portions of the paper that are shaded gray.

4 Open the paper, and you will get a butterfly.

A FLOWER

1 Fold the colored paper in half to form a triangle as seen in the diagram.

2 Fold the two bottom ends of the paper upward in order to form a square.

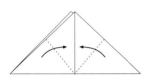

3 Fold the two sides of the square toward the center to form a diamond shape as shown.

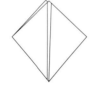

4 Fold the "diamond" in half so you get a triangle. Cut away the top of the triangle as shown.

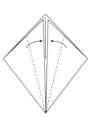

5 Trace the pattern on the right onto the triangle.

6 Using the scissors, carefully cut away the portions of the paper that are shaded gray.

7 Open the paper, and you will get a beautiful flower design.

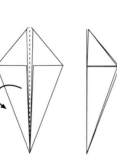

EID-E-FETR

The last day of Ramezan is known as Eid-e-Fetr in Iran. On this day is held one of the biggest events observed by Muslims all around the world.

The ninth month of the Islamic calendar is called Ramezan in Iran. It is also the month Muslims around the world (both Shi'ite and Sunni) fast every day from dawn until dusk.

Ramezan begins when the new moon, or the thinnest crescent of the moon, appears. The month of Ramezan lasts for thirty days. Eid-e-Fetr is the first day of the following month and is widely celebrated. It is one of the days in the Islamic calendar on which fasting is not allowed. Eid-e-Fetr is a big event for Muslims, although other Muslims living outside Iran sometimes refer to it by different names.

All Muslims regard the period of fasting as a time of discipline, self-control, and obedience to God's commands. All Muslims who have reached the age of *mukallaf* are expected to fast. Exceptions are made only for pregnant women, people who are ill, those who are traveling, and the elderly. Apart from the elderly or the very ill, people are expected to make up later in the year for lost days when they did not fast.

During the month of Ramezan Muslims do not eat or drink from sunrise to sunset. A fasting Muslim also avoids lying, arguing, or speaking ill of others. It is a time to make amends, reflect, and be charitable. Muslims are also expected to read the Qur'an's thirty chapters, one chapter a day.

At the start of every fasting day Muslims wake up before dawn and have a meal, which is called *Sahari*

In Iran Eftaar, or the breaking of the fast, usually starts with some dates and a cup of tea.

in Farsi. They then say the morning prayers before beginning to fast at the crack of dawn. The fast must be broken at sunset each day, and this ritual is called *Eftaar*. Iranians sometimes gather in a cafe near where they live or at a close friend's home to break fast with others.

The night before Eid-e-Fetr every Iranian is expected to give *fetrieh*, or a donation, to the poor. Traditionally, a small sack of rice or wheat is given. Recently, Iranians can also choose to give a sum of money equal to the value of the bag of grain. Some Iranians prefer to give their donations to mosques for distribution to the poor.

This miniature painting shows a scene from traditional life when the people hunted game for sport. Although most people today lead a modern life, many old customs related to celebrations are still followed.

It is also customary for Iranians to stay in their own homes on the eve of Eid-e-Fetr. That is because the amount of *fetrieh* each household contributes is determined by the number of people under their roof that night. Tradition has it that if an Iranian visits another person on this night, then the visitor's *fetrieh* is borne by the head of the household they

As part of the Eid-e-Fetr tradition, wealthier Muslims are expected to give either a sum of money or a bag of grain to the poor and needy.

have visited. So, Iranians make it a strict point to stay in their own homes on the eve of Eid-e-Fetr, so that they can pay their own *fetrieh*.

Eid-e-Fetr marks the end of Ramezan. In Iran people gather at mosques for morning prayers before visiting family and friends. A wide variety of food is served and eaten during these visits.

Iranians greet each other with *"Eid-e-fetr mobarak."* This phrase wishes the other person a happy Eid-e-Fetr.

SIMURGH: THE KING OF BIRDS

Stories of Simurgh have been passed down from generation to generation since ancient times. Although there are several descriptions of Simurgh, everyone agrees that he is a magnificent, griffinlike creature with magical powers.

IN MANY ACCOUNTS Simurgh is said to have the head and body of an eagle, a human face, orange feathers, two pairs of wings, and long tail feathers. Simurgh's tail feathers are supposed to be prettier than those of a peacock. When fanned out, Simurgh's tail feathers show marvelous designs and glow brighter than any rainbow. Since Simurgh has seen the world destroyed and rebuilt three times over, he possesses wisdom drawn from lessons learned over time.

Many years ago Simurgh once saved a special baby boy. The baby Zaal was the son of Saum, the ruler of Sistan, an ancient region in southeastern Iran. For many years Saum was unhappy because he was childless and badly longed for a child. Not surprisingly, Saum was very excited when Zaal was born. But laying eyes on the newborn made Saum even more unhappy. Zaal had a beautiful face and flawless skin, but he also had a head of snow-white hair, a very bad omen, or sign, for ancient Persians. To avoid any misfortune or curse, Saum ordered his servants to leave Zaal at the foot of faraway Mount Alburz.

Simurgh lived on the peak of Mount Alburz, a place beyond people's reach. Looking down from his nest, Simurgh noticed the baby and adopted him. Simurgh raised Zaal to become a powerful warrior, and Zaal grew his hair long. News of Zaal's remarkable strength and looks soon spread across the land.

For many years Saum believed that Zaal had died soon after birth. But Saum discovered the truth one day and sought to reunite with his now mighty son. Saum tried to scale Mount Alburz but always failed. Still, Saum never gave up. Simurgh felt sorry for him and finally told Zaal to return to his father. Simurgh gave Zaal a feather and told him to burn the feather when he was in dire trouble and Simurgh would come to his rescue.

When Zaal returned to Sistan, Saum made his son the new ruler. Some time later Zaal married Rudabeh. Astrologers had predicted that their child would become a legendary conqueror. When it was time for Rudabeh to give birth, she became ill and showed no sign of recovery. Zaal was very upset and decided to burn Simurgh's feather.

True to his word, Simurgh appeared. With his wisdom Simurgh told Zaal how to save Rudabeh and their unborn child. Rostam, the son of Zaal and Rudabeh, did indeed grow up to become a strong and fearless warrior.

ASHURA

All Shi'ite Muslims observe this solemn period during Moharram, the first month of the Islamic calendar. It is a time for religious reflection.

The ninth and tenth days of the month of Moharram are a very solemn period for Shi'ite Muslims called *Ashura*.

At Ashura Iranians mourn the tragic death of Imam Hossein, the third *imam*, and also remember and honor his sacrifices. Imam Hossein was the second son of Imam Ali, Prophet Muhammad's son-in-law.

In Iran the month of Moharram, and not just Ashura, is marked with various mournful events. One of these events is *Ta'ziyeh*. It is a reenactment of the events leading up to Imam Hossein's death.

The reenactment is based on the Battle of Karbala, which took place over a thousand years ago. After the death of Prophet Muhammad the Islamic community in the Middle East began to break up. It split into smaller groups that were locked in power struggles to gain the top leadership, called the caliphate. Over time the squabbling grew into friction between two main groups: the Sunnis and the Shi'ites.

The Shi'ites believed that only descendants of the prophet could take on the caliphate, while the Sunnis accepted leaders who need not be related to the prophet. Because the prophet did not have a son, the Shi'ites regarded his son-in-law, Imam Ali, as the rightful successor.

Ali was assassinated, and the Umayyad dynasty representing the Sunnis took over the caliphate. In A.D. 680, 20 years after his father Ali's death, Hossein was so moved by support from the people of Kufah, Iraq, that he led

28

While prayer beads are used by both Sunni and Shi'ite Muslims, Shi'ite Muslims also use a prayer stone, which they press against their forehead when kneeling in prayer.

his family from Mecca in Saudi Arabia toward Kufah, where he was to become their leader.

Hossein and his family, however, never made it to Kufah. The Umayyads sent soldiers into the desert to attack Hossein. Hossein and his family were tortured and killed near Karbala in Iraq. Karbala is regarded by the Shi'ites as a holy city today.

Iranians wear black as a sign of mourning during Moharram. All forms of entertainment stop.

Ashura, the tenth day in the month, is the peak period of mourning. It is common to see Iranians sobbing openly. Contrary to many silent mourning ceremonies in keeping with the Iranian tradition, Moharram sees people in the streets reading aloud stories about Iman Hossein.

SHARBAT-E ALBALOO

This drink made from cherry syrup is usually served during sad religious festivals.

YOU WILL NEED
1 ¾ lbs pitted cherries
6 fl. ounces water
5 lbs sugar
2 fl. ounces rose water
3 cardamom seeds

Method

1 In a large pot mix the pitted cherries, water, and sugar, and bring to a boil on the stove.

2 Once the water is boiling, add the rose water and cardamom seeds. Turn the heat down, and maintain a simmer for one hour.

3 At the end of the hour you will get a thick cherry jam and syrup. Separate the jam from the syrup.

4 Add 3 teaspoons of cherry syrup to water and ice for a refreshing drink. The cherry jam can be stored and be used as a spread.

OTHER FESTIVALS

Many of the celebrations in Iran are of Islamic origin and are based on the Iranian calendar.

Eid-e Ghadir is a religious holiday that falls on the eighteenth day of Zihajj, the twelfth and last month of the Islamic calendar.

Although Eid-e Ghadir is an Islamic holiday, it is only observed by Shi'ite Muslims. For the Shi'ites Eid-e Ghadir marks the day Prophet Muhammad appointed Imam Ali to be his successor. The prophet selected Imam Ali in front of the people at Ghadir-e-Khumm, an area in western Saudi Arabia. That is why the festival is also sometimes called Eid-e Ghadire Khumm.

In Iran descendants of the prophet are known as Say-yeds. On the day of Eid-e Ghadir Say-yeds wear green clothes because green is the color of Islam, and they stay at home the whole day to receive visitors. Say-yeds often offer visitors a sweet called *Noghle*. Iranians believe that it will bring good luck. Some Say-yeds also give gold coins or other expensive items to their close family members and friends.

Eid-e Ghorban is a festival celebrating Prophet Ibrahim's unshakable trust and faith in God, Allah. It takes place during the last month of the lunar calendar.

Ibrahim was a good man who went through much suffering in his early life. He was abandoned by his family and friends, driven out of his home country, and even thrown into a fire. All of these tragedies put together, however, did not lessen Ibrahim's faith.

In the end, God tested Ibrahim by asking him to kill his son, Ismail. Just as Ibrahim was about to strike, God stopped him. God was satisfied that Ibrahim's trust in Him was complete. God then gave Ibrahim a ram to kill instead of his son.

Today, Haji Muslims, or those who have made a pilgrimage to Mecca, sacrifice a sheep or ram on Eid-e Ghorban to honor the greatness of Ibrahim's love for God. In Iran most people hire a butcher to slaughter the animal in front of their house.

In the Islamic world this act of sacrificing an animal and then sharing the meat with others who are less fortunate is considered holy.

WORDS TO KNOW

Descendants: Family members who are born after the person being mentioned.

Equinox: The two times a year when the Sun crosses the Earth's equator, making day and night last for the same number of hours.

Farsi: The language of Persia since A.D. 900; it is written in Arabic script.

Haji Firouz: The Iranian version of Santa Claus. He is dressed in red and has a black face.

Imam: The title for a Muslim leader or chief.

Mukallaf: A Muslim who has reached the age when he or she can tell the difference between right and wrong, and who can take responsibility for his or her actions.

Mythical: An imaginary object that does not exist.

Pomegranate: A round fruit with a reddish-colored skin. It has many small white seeds and has a juicy taste.

Prophet Muhammad: The final prophet appointed to spread the message of Islam.

Qur'an: The holy book of Islam.

Ramezan: The Muslim fasting month that lasts for thirty days. It takes place during the last month of the Islamic calendar. During this period most Muslims will not eat or drink between sunrise and sunset.

Reenactment: To re-create an event.

Shi'ite Muslims: Followers of a minority branch of Islam that is mainly observed in Iran.

Sunni Muslims: Followers of the main type of Islam. Most of the people in the world who are Muslims are Sunni Muslims.

Zoroastrianism: An Iranian religion founded around 600 B.C. by Zoroaster. Followers of this religion believe in a supreme being called Ahura Mazda and a struggle between the spirits of good and evil.

ACKNOWLEDGMENTS

WITH THANKS TO:
Selina Kuo, Jamilah Mohd Hassan, and Neda Namazie for the loan of objects and advice in the preparation of this book.

PHOTOGRAPHS BY:
Bes Stock (cover); Sam Yeo (pp.16-17, p.18 bottom left), Yu Hui Ying (all other images).

ILLUSTRATIONS BY:
Ang Lee Ming (p. 1, p. 5 top), Amy Ong (p. 4), Enrico Sallustio (p. 5 middle and bottom, p. 7), Lee Kowling (p.15), Ong Lay Keng (p. 27).

Set Contents